GIVE ME LIBERTY

BY

ROSE WILDER LANE

LONGMANS, GREEN AND CO.

NEW YORK · TORONTO

1936

Part of this book appeared
in the *Saturday Evening Post*
in the article entitled "Credo"

GIVE ME LIBERTY

Sixteen years ago I was a communist. My Bolshevik friends of those days are scattered now; some are bourgeois, some are dead, some are in China and Russia, and by chance I have not met the new American chiefs of the Third International. They would repudiate me even as a renegade comrade, for I was never a member of The Party. But it was merely an accident that I was not.

In those days immediately after the war, it was not prudent to advocate fundamental changes in America. The cry was, "If you don't like this country, go back where you came from!" I had friends, patriotic Americans from American families as old as my own, who had been tried and sentenced to twenty years' imprisonment for editing a magazine friendly to the Russian experiment. Ships lay with steam up and papers cleared, ready to whisk from these shores, without legal process or any opportunity for defense, groups of suspected radicals rounded up by agents of the Department of Justice. Policemen were breaking down unlocked doors, smashing innocent furniture and, with a surprising lack of discrimination, beating up Russian immigrants.

Amid all this hysteria and in quite real danger, Jack Reed was organizing the Communist Party in America.

I forget the precise locale of that historic scene, but I was there. Somewhere in the slums of New York, a dirty stairway went up from the filthy sidewalk. Haggard urchins at the door offered Communist publications for sale. The usual gaunt women were asking help for someone's legal defense. "A dime, comrade? A nickel? Every penny counts now."

We went up through the sluggish jostling on the stairs to the usual dingy room with the rented chairs, the slightly crooked posters on smudged walls, the smell of poverty and the hungry, lighted faces.

All those meetings were the same, that winter. Their light seemed to come, not from the grudging bulbs that dangled from the ceiling, but from the faces. Our police were shouting that Communists were foreigners, and it was true that most of the faces were foreign, and many of the voices. But these people had a vision that seemed to me the American dream. They had followed it to America and they were still following it; a dream of a new world of freedom, justice and equality.

They had escaped from oppression in Europe, to exist in New York's slums, to work endless hours in sweat shops and wearily study English at night. They were hungry and exhausted and exploited by their own people in this strange land, and to their dream of a better world which they did not hope to live long enough to see, they gave the dimes they needed for food.

I remember the room as a small room, with perhaps sixty men and women in it. There was an almost unbearable sense of expectancy, and a sense of danger. The meeting had not begun. A few men gathered around Jack Reed were talking earnestly, urgently. He caught sight of the man with me, and his tenseness broke into Jack Reed's smile, more joyous than a shout. He broke loose from the others, reached us in half a dozen strides and exclaimed, "Are you with us!"

"Are you?" he repeated, expectant. But the question itself was a challenge. This was a risky enterprise. Jack Reed, as every Communist knows, did not leave his own country later; he escaped from it. Federal agents, raiding police, might break in upon us at that moment. We knew this, and because I shared the Communist dream I was prepared to take risks and also to submit to the rigorous Party discipline. But the man beside me began a vague discussion of tactics; evaded; hesitated; questioned and demurred; finally, with a disarming smile, doubted whether he should risk committing himself, his safety was so valuable to The Cause. Jack Reed turned on his heel, saying, "Oh, go to hell, you damn coward."

This brief scene had shown me my complete unimportance at the moment; I represented no group, carried no weight in that complex of theorists and of leaders. I was merely an individual, just then heartily in sympathy with Jack Reed's words, and dazed by a miserable cold. I went home. The cold proved to be influenza; I nearly died, expenses overwhelmed me, I had to make my living, and before my health recovered I was in Europe.

By so narrow a margin I was not a member of the Communist Party. Nevertheless, I was at heart a communist.

Many regard Communism, as I did, as an extension of democracy. In this view, the picture is one of progressive steps to freedom. The first step was the Reformation; that won freedom of conscience. The second was the political revolution; our American revolution against an English king was part of that. This second step won for all western peoples varying degrees of political freedom. Liberals have continued to increase that freedom by giving increasing political power to the people. In the United States, for example, Liberals gained equal suffrage, popular election of nearly all public officials, initiative, referendum, recall, and the primaries.

But now, we confront economic tyranny. Stated in its simplest terms, no man is free whose very livelihood can be denied him at another man's will. The worker is a wage-slave. The final revolution, then, must capture economic control.

I now see a dominant fallacy in that picture, and I shall point it out. But let it pass for the moment. There is another picture. This:

Since the progress of science and invention enables us to produce more goods than we can consume, no one should lack any material thing. Yet we see on the one hand, great wealth in the hands of a few who, owning and controlling all means of production, own all the goods produced; on the other hand, we see multitudes always relatively poor, lacking goods they should enjoy.

Who owns this great wealth? The Capitalist.
What creates wealth? Labor. How does the Capitalist get it? He collects a profit on all goods produced. Does the Capitalist produce anything? No;
Labor produces everything. Then, if all working
men, organized in trade-unions, compelled all capi-
talists to pay in wages the full value of their labor,
they could buy all the goods produced? No, because the Capitalist adds his profit to the goods before
he sells them.

From this point of view, it is clear that the Profit
System causes the injustice, the inequality, we see.
We must eliminate profit; that is to say, we must
eliminate the Capitalist. We will take his current
profits, distribute his accumulated wealth, and ourselves administer his former affairs. The workers
who produce the goods will then enjoy all the goods,
there will no longer be any economic inequality, and
we shall have such general prosperity as the world has
never known.

When the Capitalist is gone, who will manage production? The State. And what is The State?
The State will be the mass of the toiling workers.

It was at this point that the first doubt pierced my
Communist faith.

II

I was in Transcaucasian Russia at the time, drinking
tea with cherry preserves in it and trying to hold a
lump of sugar between my teeth while I did so. It's
difficult. My plump Russian hostess and her placid,

golden-bearded husband beamed at me, and a number
of round-cheeked children stared in wonder at the
American. Their house was a century old, and
charming. Icons hung on thick walls whiter than
snow; featherbeds rounded upward in the bed-niche
of the large stove, which was also white-washed.
Almost everything was embroidered; my host's
collar and his wife's gown were works of art. There
was an American sewing machine, and the samovar
was a proud samovar.

The village was communist, of course; it had always been communist. The sole source of wealth
was land, and it had never occurred to these villagers
that land could be privately owned.

These plains of Russian Georgia are a great deal
like those of Illinois. The Russians came into them
as pioneers about the same time that Americans were
moving into Illinois. Industrious, thrifty, good-na-
tured and eminently sensible people, they moved in
groups, settled in villages, cultivated the good land in
common, and prospered.

The land was free. Each village cultivated as much
as it needed. Within the village, each family tilled
an allotted acreage. When in the course of natural
events, the size of the families altered so that the division of land was unsatisfactory, all the villagers assembled in town-meeting and wrangled out a new
division. This happened every ten years or so, de-
pending on births, marriages and deaths.

These people had never been oppressed by land-
owners; most of the villages had no experience of
land owners and none of them had had any real con-

tact with the Czar's government. Once a year, in the fall, they had been accustomed to paying a tax-collector a small percentage of the year's yield from the grain-fields. The tax-collector came riding across the plains, collected the taxes in an ox-wagon, and rode away. The young men occasionally went to war, usually to a little private war with a Tartar village. Most of these Russians were primitive Christians, opposed to war; they had come, or had been driven, from Old Russia because they would not send their sons to the Czar's armies. But with the passing of a century their opposition had weakened; the young men had sometimes been willing enough to be conscripted for war. Thus, occasionally, an officer rode into the village, young men rode away with him, and when they returned months or years later they brought the news of where they had been and what they had done and seen.

I had before me the spectacle of a virgin country, free land, rich soil, to which the pioneers had brought communism. They had lived here for a hundred years, undisturbed. I met in these villages many old men who asked me what had been the result in my country when the Czar of the World died. I met young men who had been in German prison camps, and who explained to pop-eyed neighbors that I came from America, a fabulous land to which you might write a letter asking for anything — for food, for cigarettes, for socks, matches, sugar, even for a coat — and it would come.

And they were not at all stupid. They were the best of farmers and dairymen, they were good mechanics; they were fine housekeepers and cooks. They were open-minded and experimental. One village had imported a Swiss, at a good salary, and built a Swiss chalet for him and his family; he was employed to raise the breed of milch cows and to make cheese in the village cheese factory. There was one village two miles long and one street wide, lighted by electricity from the village electric plant; its women did not do their washing in the river, but in a village laundry.

Crops had been good that year; the cattle were fat, the granaries overflowed, and all the open house-lofts held piles of red-gold pumpkins. Of course, there was not a poor man in the town. Everyone worked, and — weather permitting — everyone who worked was abundantly fed. No communist could have desired better proof of Communism's practical value than the prosperous well-being of those villagers.

The Bolsheviks had then been nearly four years in power and the village taxes had not been increased, nor any more young men taken for the army than during the Czar's regime. These villages depended hardly at all upon Tiflis, the nearest city, but even Tiflis was at the moment reviving under NEP, Lenin's New Economic Policy of a temporary breathing spell for capitalism.

My host astounded me by the force with which he said that he did not like the new government. I could hardly believe that a lifelong communist, with the proofs of successful communism thick about us, was opposed to a communist government. He repeated that he did not like it. "No! No!"

His complaint was government interference with village affairs. He protested against the growing bureaucracy that was taking more and more men from productive work. He predicted chaos and suffering from the centralizing of economic power in Moscow. These were not his words, but that was what he meant.

This, I said to myself, is the opposition of the peasant mind to new ideas, too large for him to grasp. Here is my small opportunity to spread a little light. I could understand simple Russian, but I could not speak it well, and through my interpreter I explained in primer words the parallel between the village land, as a source of wealth, and all sources of wealth. I drew for him a picture of Great Russia, to its remotest corner enjoying the equality, the peace and the justly divided prosperity of his village. He shook his head sadly.

"It is too big," he said. "Too big. At the top, it is too small. It will not work. In Moscow there are only men, and man is not God. A man has only a man's head, and one hundred heads together do not make one great head. No. Only God can know Russia."

A westerner among Russians often suddenly feels that they are all slightly mad. At other times, their mysticism seems plain common sense. It is quite true that many heads do not make one great head; actually, they make a session of Congress. What, then, I asked myself dizzily, is The State? The Communist State — does it exist? Can it exist?

I wonder now whether that ancestral home, that

village, have yet been wiped from the soil of Russia to make way for a communal farm, worked in three daily eight-hour shifts, plowed by tractors and harvested by combines, illuminated at night by enormous arc-lights. Do my host and his wife eat, perhaps, in a communal dining hall and sleep in communal barracks?

Certainly their standard of living was primitive. In a hundred years, it had not changed. They had no electric lights, no plumbing. They bathed, I supposed, only once a week, in the village bath-house, and perhaps it wasn't sanitary. How many germs were in their drinking water, no one knew. Their windows were not screened. Their dusty roads were undoubtedly fathomless mud in rainy weather. They had no automobiles, nor even horses; only ox-wagons. Their standard of living, in a word, was that of the pioneers in Illinois a hundred years ago. Possibly their standard of living has already been raised. It may be that in time every tooth in Russia will be brushed thrice daily and every child fed spinach.

But if this is done for the people in former Russia, it will not be done by them, but to them. And what will do it? The State?

III

THE picture of the economic revolution as the final step to freedom was false as soon as I asked myself that question. For, in actual fact, The State, The Government, cannot exist. They are abstract concepts, useful enough in their place, as the theory of minus numbers is useful in mathematics. In actual living experience, however, it is impossible to subtract anything from nothing; when a purse is empty, it is empty, it cannot contain a minus ten dollars. On this same plane of actuality, no State, no Government, exists. What does in fact exist is a man, or a few men, in power over many men.

The Reformation reduced the power of priests, so that common men were free to think and to speak as they pleased. Political revolution reduced or destroyed the power of kings, so that common men were more nearly free to do as they pleased. But economic revolution concentrated economic power in the hands of rulers, so that the lives, the livelihoods, of common men were once more subject to dictators.

Every advance toward personal liberty which had been gained by the religious revolution and by the political revolution, was lost by the economic revolution.

When I considered facts, I could not see how it could be otherwise. The communist village was possible because there a few men, face to face, struggled each for his own self-interest, until out of that conflict a reasonably satisfactory balance was arrived at. The same thing happens within every family. But the government of men in hundreds of millions is another thing. Time and space prevent a personal struggle of so many wills, each in personal encounter with each of the others arriving at a common decision. The government of multitudes of men must be in the hands of a few men.

Americans blamed Lenin because he did not establish a republic. Had he done so, the fact that a few men ruled Russia would not have been altered.

Representative government cannot express the will of the mass of the people, because there is no mass of the people; The People is a fiction, like The State. You can not get a Will of the Mass, even among a dozen persons who all want to go on a picnic. The only human mass with a common will is a mob, and that will is a temporary insanity. In actual fact, the population of a country is a multitude of diverse human beings with an infinite variety of purposes and desires and fluctuating wills.

In a republic, a majority of this population from time to time directs, checks, or changes its rulers. From time to time, an action of a majority can alter the methods by which men get power, the extent of that power, or the terms upon which they are allowed to keep it. But a majority does not govern; it can not govern; it acts as a check on its governors. Any government of multitudes of men, anywhere, at any time, must be a man, or few men, in power. There is no way to escape from that fact.

A republic is not possible in the Soviet Union because the aim of its rulers is an economic aim. Economic power differs from political power.

Politics is a matter of broad principles which, once adopted, may stand unchanged indefinitely; such principles as, for example, that government derives its just powers from the consent of the governed. From such principles are drawn general rules; as, no taxation without representation. Such rules are embodied

in law governing action; as, The sole right to levy
taxes is vested in Congress and only Congress may
spend the collected tax-money. This most concrete
application of political principle does not touch the
intimate detail of an individual's life. We may carelessly give Congress its head, we may neglect to jerk
back sharply on the bit, we may yip when we have to
borrow money to pay our taxes, or we may lose our
farm or house if we can't, and still our personal freedom of choice is ours.

Economics, however, is not concerned with abstract
principles and general laws, but with material things;
it deals directly with actual carloads of coal, harvests
of grain, output of factories. Economic power in
action is subject to an infinity of immediately unpredictable crises affecting material things; it is subject
to drought, storm, flood, earthquake and pestilence, to
fashion, and diseases, and insects, to the breaking
down and the wearing out of machinery. And economics enters into the minute detail of each person's
existence — into his eating, drinking, working, playing,
and personal habits.

Economic rulers must settle such questions as:
How many yards of cloth shall be used in a woman's
dress? Shall lipsticks be permitted? Is there any
economic value in chewing-gum? There is a perfectly good point of view, from which the whole
tobacco industry is an economic waste.

The entire economic circulation-system of a modern country is affected by the number of its people
who wash behind the ears. This somewhat private
matter affects the import and production of vegetable

oils; the use of fat from farm animals; the manufacture of chemicals, perfumes, colors; the building or closing of soap factories, with attendant changes in employment in these factories and in the building trades and heavy industries, and in the demand for raw materials and for labor in their production; and freight-car loadings, and use of fuel, with its effects on mines, oilfields and transportation. So much for soap; consider now the washcloth, to be used or not to be used, with all the effects of that decision upon cotton fields, or flax, and labor, in field and in factory, cotton-gins with their by-product of cottonseed for oil or fertilizer or stock-feed, and spinning and weaving machines, their demands on the steel industry.

All these economic factors and many others change with changing habits of personal cleanliness. A Hollywood diet or a passion for jigsaw puzzles has prodigious results in the most unexpected, remote places. Whether the hungry child home from school eats bread and butter or candy is a matter of international economic importance.

Centralized economic control over multitudes of human beings must therefore be continuous and perhaps superhumanly flexible, and it must be autocratic. It must be government by a swift flow of edicts issued in haste to catch up with events receding into the past before they can be reported, arranged, analyzed and considered, and it will be compelled to use compulsion. In the effort to succeed, it must become such minute and rigorous control of details of individual life as no people will accept without compulsion. It cannot be subject to the intermittent checks, reversals, and removals of men in power which majorities cause in republics.

IV

IN RUSSIA, then, our hope was realized; the economic revolution had occurred. The Communist Party had captured power with the cry, "All power to the councils!"

Russia's embryo capitalism was in reality destroyed, and the people controlled the national wealth. That is to say, in actual fact a sincere and extremely able and intelligent man was in power, devoted to the stupendous task of reducing multitudes of human beings to efficient economic order, for what this man and his followers honestly believed to be the ultimate material welfare of those multitudes.

And what I saw was not an extension of human freedom, but the establishment of tyranny on a new, widely extended and deeper base.

The historical novelty in the Soviet government is its motive. Other governments have existed to keep peace among their subjects, or to amass money from them, or to use them in trade and war for the glory of the men governing them. But the Soviet government exists to do good to its people, whether they like it or not.

And I felt that, of all the tyrannies to which men have been subject, that tyranny would be the most ruthless and the most agonizing to bear. There is some refuge for freedom under other tyrannies, since they are less thorough and not so remorselessly armed with righteousness. But from benevolence in economic power I could see no refuge whatever.

Every report I have since heard from the Soviet Union has confirmed this opinion, and I listen only to reports from its friends, for I believe that Communists best understand what is happening there.

For nineteen years the men who rule that country have toiled prodigiously to create precisely the society we dreamed of; a society in which insecurity, poverty, economic inequality, shall be impossible.

To that end they have destroyed personal freedom; freedom of movement, of choice of work, freedom of self-expression in ways of life, freedom of speech, freedom of conscience.

Given their aim, I do not see how they could have done otherwise. Producing food from the earth and the sea, making goods from assembled raw materials, and their storing, exchanging, transporting, distributing and consuming by vast multitudes of human beings, are activities so intricately inter-related and interdependent that efficient control of any part of them demands control of the whole. No man can so control multitudes of men without compulsion, and that compulsion must increase.

It must increase because human beings are naturally diverse. It is the nature of men to do the same thing in different ways, to waste time and energy in altering the shapes of things, to experiment, invent, make mistakes, depart from the past in an infinite variety of directions. Plants and animals repeat routine, but men who are not restrained will go into the future like explorers into a new country, and exploration is always wasteful. Great numbers of explorers accomplish nothing and many are lost.

Economic compulsion is, therefore, constantly threatened by human wilfulness. It must constantly overcome that wilfulness, crush all impulses of egotism and independence, destroy variety of human desires and behavior. Centralized economic power endeavoring to plan and to control the economic processes of a modern nation is under a necessity, either to fail, or to tend to become absolute power in every province of human life.

"It doesn't matter what happens to individuals," the communists say. "Individuals don't matter. The only thing that matters is the collectivist State."

The Communist hope of economic equality in the Soviet Union rests now on the death of all men and women who are individuals. A new generation, they tell me, had already been so shaped and schooled that a human Mass is actually being created; millions of young men and women do, in veritable fact, have the psychology of the bee swarm, the anthill.

This does not seem so incredible to me as it once did. There may yet be a human bee-swarm in Russia. It would not be unique in history; there was Sparta.

There was Sparta, unchanging in its rigid forms of standardized behavior and thought until it was destroyed from without. There is the bee-swarm, static, unchanging through untold generations of individuals who ceaselessly repeat the same pattern of action devoted to the welfare of all. If there is progress in life, that is not life; it is a kind of animate and breathing death.

v

I CAME out of the Soviet Union no longer a communist, because I believed in personal freedom. Like all Americans, I took for granted the individual liberty to which I had been born. It seemed as necessary and as inevitable as the air I breathed; it seemed the natural element in which human beings lived.

The thought that I might lose it had never remotely occurred to me. And I could not conceive that multitudes of human beings would ever willingly live without it.

It happened that I spent many years in the countries of Europe and Western Asia, so that at last I learned something, not only of the words that various peoples speak, but of the real meanings of those words. No word, of course, is ever exactly translatable into another language; the words we use are the most clumsy symbols for meanings, and to suppose that such words as "war," "glory," "justice," "Liberty," "home," mean the same in two languages, is an error.

Everywhere in Europe I encountered the living facts of medieval caste and of the static medieval social order. I saw them resisting, and vitally resisting, democracy and the industrial revolution.

It was impossible for me to know France without, I thought, knowing that the French demand order, discipline, the restraint of traditional forms, and that the fierce French democracy is not a cry for individual liberty but an insistence that the upper classes of citizens shall not unduly exploit the lower.

I thought I saw in Germany and in Austria scattered and leaderless sheep running this way and that, longing for the lost security of the flock and the shepherd.

Resisting step by step, I was finally compelled to admit to my Italian friends that I had seen the spirit of Italy revive under Mussolini. And it seemed to me that this revival was based on a separation of democracy, of individual liberty, from the industrial revolution that had accompanied the rise of individual freedom. I said that in Italy, as in Russia, an essentially medieval, planned and controlled economic order was taking over the fruits of the industrial revolution without yielding to the principle of the rights of the individual.

"Why *will* you talk about the rights of individuals!" Italians exclaimed, at last impatient. "Individuals don't matter. As individuals we have no importance whatever. I will die, you will die, millions will live and die, but Italy does not die. Italy is important. Nothing matters but Italy."

This rejection of one's self as an individual was, I knew, the spirit animating the members of the Communist Party. I heard that it was the spirit beginning to animate Russia. It was the spirit of Fascism, the spirit that indubitably did revive Italy. Scores, hundreds of the smallest incidents revealed it.

In 1920, Italy was a fleas' nest of beggars and thieves. They fell on the stranger and devoured him. There was no instant in which baggage could be left

unguarded; every bill was an over-charge and no
service however small was unaccompanied by a bill;
taxis dodged into vacant streets and boats stopped
midway to ships, that drivers and boatmen might ter-
rorize timid passengers into paying twice. Every
step in Italy was a wrangle and a fight.

In 1927, my car broke down after nightfall in the
edge of a small Italian village.   Three men, a waiter,
a charcoal burner, and the uniformed chauffeur of
wealthy travelers sleeping in the inn, worked all night
on the engine.   When it was running smoothly in the
bleak dawn, all three refused to take any payment.
Americans in a similiar situation would have refused
from democratic kindness and personal pride.   The
Italians said firmly, "No, signora. We did it for
Italy."   This was typical.   Italians were no longer
centered in themselves, but in that mythical creation
of their imaginations unto which they poured their
lives, Italy, immortal Italy.

I began at last to question the value of this personal
freedom which had seemed so inherently right.   I
saw how rare it is.   From Brittany to Basra I considered the ruins of brilliant civilizations whose peoples
had never glimpsed the idea that men are born free.
In sixty centuries of human history that idea did not
appear.

It has been a familiar idea to only a few men on
earth, for little more than two centuries.   Asia did
not know it.   Africa did not know it.   Europe had
never wholly accepted it, and was now rejecting it.

I began to question, What is individual liberty?

VI

WHEN I asked myself, "Am I truly free?" of course I saw at once that I am not. The most that can be said is that, being American, I have a relative freedom.

Americans have more freedom of thought, of choice, and of movement than other peoples have ever had. We inherited no limitations of caste to restrict our range of desires and of ambition to the class in which we were born.

We had no governmental bureaucracy to watch our every move, to make a record of friends who called at our homes and the hours at which they arrived and left, in order that the police might be fully informed in case we were murdered. We had no officials who, in the interests of a just and equitable collection of gasoline taxes, stopped our cars and measured the gasoline in the tanks whenever we entered or left an American city.

We are not obliged, as Continental Europeans are, to carry at all times a police card, renewed and paid for at intervals, bearing our pictures properly stamped and stating our names, ages, addresses, parentage, religion and occupation.

American workers are not classified; they do not carry police cards on which employers record each day they work; they have no places of amusement separate from those of higher classes, and their amusements are not subject to interruption by raiding policemen inspecting their workingmen's cards and acting on the assumption that any workingman is a thief whose card shows he has not worked during the past week.

In 1922, as a foreign correspondent in Budapest, I accompanied such a police raid. The Chief of Police was showing the mechanisms of his work to a visiting operative from Scotland Yard. We set out at ten o'clock at night, leading sixty policemen who moved with the beautiful precision of soldiers.

They surrounded a section of the workingmen's quarter of the city and closed in, while the Chief explained that this was ordinary routine; the whole quarter was combed in this way every week.

We appeared suddenly in the doorways of workingmen's cafes, dingy places with sawdust on earthen floors where one musician forlornly tried to make music on a cheap fiddle and men and women in the gray rags of poverty sat at bare tables and economically sipped beer or coffee. Their terror at the sight of uniforms was abject. All rose and meekly raised their hands. The policemen grinned with that peculiar enjoyment of human beings in possessing such power.

They went through the men's pockets, making some little jest at this object and that. They found the Labor cards, inspected them, thrust them back in the pockets. At their curt word of release, the men dropped into chairs and wiped their foreheads.

In every place, a few cards failed to pass the examination. No employer had stamped them during the past three days. Men and women were loaded into the patrol wagon.

Now and then, at our entrance, someone tried to

escape from back door or window and ran, of course, into the clutch of policemen. We could hear the policemen laughing. The Chief accepted the compliments of the British detective. Everything was perfectly done; no one escaped.

Several women frantically protested, crying, pleading on their knees, so that they had almost to be carried to the wagon. One young girl fought, screaming horribly. It took two policemen to handle her; they were not rough, but when she bit at their hands on her arms, a third slapped her face. In the wagon she went on screaming insanely. I could not understand Hungarian. The Chief explained that some women objected to being given prostitute's cards.

When a domestic servant had been several days without work, the police took away the card that identified her as a working girl and permitted her to work; they gave her instead a prostitute's card. Men who had not worked recently were sentenced to a brief imprisonment for theft. Obviously, the Chief said, if they were not working, they were prostitutes and thieves; how else were they living?

Perhaps on their savings? I suggested.

Working people make only enough to live on from day to day, they can not save, the Chief said. Of course, if by any remarkable chance one of them had got some money honestly and could prove it, the judge would release him.

Having gone through all the cafes, we began on the tenements. I have lived in the slums of New York and of San Francisco. Americans who have not seen

European slums have not the slightest idea of what slums are.

Until dawn, the police were clambering through those filthy tenements and down into their basements, stirring up masses of rags and demanding from staring faces their police cards. We did not capture so many unemployed there, because it costs more to sleep under a roof than to sit in a cafe; the very fact that these people had any shelter argued that they were working. But the police were thorough and awakened everyone. They were quiet and good-humored; this raid had none of the violence of an American police raid. When a locked door was not opened, the police tried all their master keys before they set their shoulders to the door and went in.

The Scotland Yard man said, "Admirable, sir, admirable. Continental police systems are marvelous, really. You have absolute control over here." Then his British pride spoke, deprecatingly, as it always speaks. "We could never do anything like this in London, don't you know. An Englishman's home is his castle, and all that. We have to have a warrant before we can search the premises or touch a man's person. Beastly handicap, you know. We have nothing like your control over here on the Continent."

This is the only police search of workingmen's quarters that I saw in Europe. I do not believe that regimentation elsewhere went so far as to force unemployed women into prostitution, and it may be that it no longer does so in Hungary. But that the systematic surrounding and searching of workingmen's

quarters goes on everywhere in Europe, and that unemployment is assumed to push them over the edge
of destitution into crime, I do know.

Like everyone else domiciled in Europe, I have
many times been stopped on my way home by two
courteous policemen who asked to see my identifica-
tion card. This became too commonplace to need
explanation. I knew that my thoroughly respectable,
middle-class quarter was surrounded, simply as a matter of police routine, and that everyone in it was being
required to show police cards.

Nevertheless, I question whether there is less
crime in police-controlled Europe than in America.
Plenty of crimes are reported in brief paragraphs of
small type in every paper. There is no section of an
American city which I would fear to go into alone
at night. There are many quarters of European cities
which are definitely dangerous after nightfall, and
whole classes of criminals who will kill any moder-
ately well-dressed man, woman or child for the
clothes alone.

The terrible thing is that the motive behind all this
supervision of the individual is a good motive, and a
rational one. How is any ruler to maintain a social
order without it?

There is a certain instinct of orderliness and of self-
preservation which enables multitudes of free human
beings to get along together after a fashion. No
crowd leaves a theatre with any efficiency, nor without discomfort, impatience and wasted time, yet we
usually reach the sidewalk without a fight. Order is
another thing. Any teacher knows that order can

not be maintained without regulation, supervision and discipline. It is a question of degree; the more rigid and autocratic the discipline, the greater the order. Any genuine social order requires, as its first fundamental, the classification, regulation and obedience of individuals. Individuals being what they are, infinitely various and willful, their obedience must be enforced.

The serious loss in a social order is in time and energy. Sitting around in waiting rooms until one can stand in line before a bureaucrat's desk seems to any American a dead loss, and living in a social order thus shortens every person's life. Outside the bureaucrat's office, too, these regulations for the public good constantly hamper every action. It is as impossible to move freely in one's daily life as it is to saunter or hasten while keeping step in a procession.

In America, commercial decrees do not hamper every clerk and customer, as they do in France, so that an extra half-hour is consumed in every department-store purchase. French merchants are as intelligent as American, but they can not install vacuum tubes and a swift accounting system in a central cashier's department. What is the use? they ask you. They would still be obliged to have every purchase recorded in writing in a ledger, in the presence of both buyer and seller, as Napoleon decreed.

It was an intelligent decree, too, when Napoleon issued it. Can French merchants change it now? It is to laugh, as they say; a phrase with no mirth in it. That decree is now entangled with a hundred years of bureaucratic complications, and besides, think how much unemployment its repeal would cause today among those weary cashiers, now dipping their pens in the prescribed ink, setting down the date and hour on a new line and asking, "Your name, madame?" writing. "Your address?" writing. "You pay cash?" writing. "You will take the purchase with you? Ah, good," writing. "Ah, I see. One reel of thread, cotton, black, what size?" writing. "You pay for it how much?" writing. "And you offer in payment — Good; one franc," writing. "From one franc, perceive, madame, I give you fifty centimes change. Good. And you are satisfied, madame?"

No one thinks how much unemployment this causes to the daily multitudes of patiently waiting customers, nor that if these clerks had never been thus employed they might today be doing something useful, something creative of wealth. Napoleon wished to stop the waste of disorganization, of cheating and quarreling, in the markets of his time. And he did so. The result is that so much of France is still fixed firmly in Napoleon's time. If he had let Frenchmen waste and quarrel, and cheat and lose, as Americans were then doing in equally primitive markets, French department stores today would no doubt be as briskly efficient and time-saving as America's.

No one who dreams of the ideal social order, the economy planned to eliminate waste and injustice, considers how much energy; how much human life, is wasted in administering and in obeying the best of regulations. No one considers how rigid such regulations become, nor that they must become rigid and resist change because their underlying purpose is to preserve men from the risks of chance and change in flowing time.

Americans have had in their own country no experience of the discipline of a social order. We speak of a better social order, when in fact we do not know what any social order is. We say that something is wrong with this system, when in fact we have no system. We use phrases learned from Europe, with no conception of the meaning of those phrases in actual living experience.

In America we do not have even universal military training, that basis of a social order, which teaches every male citizen his subservience to The State and subtracts some years from every young man's life.

An apartment lease in America is legal when it is signed; it is not necessary to take it to the police to be stamped, nor to file triplicate copies of it with the collector of internal revenue, so that for taxation purposes our incomes may be set down as ten times what we pay for rent. In economic theory, no doubt it is not proper to pay for rent more than ten percent of income, and perhaps it is economic justice that anyone so extravagant as to pay more should be fined by taxation. It is never possible to quarrel with the motives behind these bureaucracies of Europe; they are invariably excellent.

An American may look at the whole world around him and take what he wants from it, if he can. Only criminal law and his own character, abilities and luck restrain him.

That is what Europeans mean when, after a few days in this country, they exclaim, "You are so free here!" And it is the most infinite relief to an American returning after long living abroad, to be able to move from hotel to hotel, from city to city, to be able to rush into a store and buy a spool of thread, to decide at half past three to take a four o'clock train, to buy an automobile if one has the money or the credit and drive it wherever one likes, all without making any reports whatever to the government.

But anyone whose freedom has been, as mine has always been and today most urgently is, freedom to earn a living if possible, knows that this independence is another name for slavery without security. It is a slavery in which one is one's own master, and must therefore bear the double burden of toil and of responsibility.

The American pioneers phrased this clearly and bluntly. They said, "Root, hog, or die."

There can be no third alternative for the shoat let out of the pen, to go where he pleases and do what he likes. Individual liberty is individual responsibility. Whoever makes decisions is responsible for results. When common men were slaves and serfs, they obeyed and they were fed. Free men paid for their freedom by leaving that security.

The question is whether personal freedom is worth the terrible effort, the never-lifted burden, and the risks, the unavoidable risks, of self-reliance.

VII

FOR each of us, the answer to that question is a personal one. But the final answer can not be personal, for individual liberty can not long exist except among multitudes of individuals who choose it and who are willing to pay for it.

Multitudes of human beings will not do this unless their freedom is worth more than it costs, not only in value to their own souls but also in terms of the general welfare and the future of their country, which means the welfare and the future of their children.

The test of the worth of personal freedom, then, can only be its practical results in a country whose institutions and ways of life and of thought have grown from individualism. The only such country is the United States of America.

Here, on a new continent, peoples with no common tradition founded this republic on the rights of the individual. This country was the only country in the western world whose territory was largely settled and whose culture is dominated by those northwestern European races from whom the idea of individual liberty came into the world's history.

When one thinks of it, that's an odd fact. Why did this territory become American? How did it happen that those British colonists released from England spread across half this continent?

Spaniards were in Missouri before Englishmen were in Virginia or Massachusetts. French settlements were old in Illinois, French mines in Missouri were furnishing the western world with bullets,

French trading posts were in Arkansas, half a century before farmers fired on British soldiers at Lexington.

Why did Americans, spreading westward, not find a populated country, a vigorous colony to protest in France against the sale of Louisiana?

This is an important fact: Americans were the only settlers who built their houses far apart, each on his own land. America is the only country I have seen where farmers do not live today in close, safe village-groups. It is the only country I know where each person does not feel an essential, permanent solidarity with a certain class, and with a certain group within that class. The first Americans came from such groups in Europe, but they came because they were individuals rebelling against groups. Each in his own way built his own house at a distance from others in the American wilderness. This is individualism.

The natural diversity of human beings, the natural tendency of man to go into the future like an explorer finding his own way, was released in those English colonies on the Atlantic coast. Men from the British islands rushed so eagerly toward that freedom that Parliament and the King refused to open any more land for settlement; the statistics of the time proved clearly that a western expansion of the American colonies would depopulate England.

Nevertheless, before tea went overboard in Boston harbor the lawless settlers had penetrated to the crests and valleys of the Appalachians and were scouting into forbidden lands beyond.

There was no plan that the young United States should ever cover half this continent. The thought of New York and Washington lagged far behind that surge. It was the released energies of individuals that poured westward at a speed never imagined, sweeping away and overwhelming settlements of more cohesive peoples and reaching the Pacific in the time that Jefferson thought it would take to settle Ohio.

I have no illusions about the pioneers. My own people for eight generations were American pioneers, and when as a child I remembered too proudly an ancestry older than Plymouth, my mother would remind me of a great-great-uncle, jailed for stealing a cow.

The pioneers were by no means the best of Europe. In general they were trouble-makers of the lower classes, and Europe was glad to be rid of them. They brought no great amount of intelligence or culture. Their principal desire was to do as they pleased, and they were no idealists. When they could not pay their debts, they skipped out between two days. When their manners, their personal habits or their loudly expressed and usually ignorant opinions offended the gently bred, they remarked, "It's a free country, ain't it?" A frequent phrase of theirs was, "free and independent." They also said, "I'll try anything once," and, "Sure, I'll take a chance!"

They were riotous speculators; they gambled in land, in furs, in lumber and canals and settlements. They were town-lot salesmen for towns that did not yet exist and, more often than not, never did materialize. They were ignorant peasants, prospectors, self-educated teachers and lawyers, ranting politicians, printers, lumberjacks, horse thieves and cattle rustlers.

Each was out to get what he could for himself, and devil take the hindmost. At every touch of adversity they fell apart, each on his own; there was human pity and kindness, but not a trace of community spirit. The pioneer had horse sense, and card sense, and money sense, but not a particle of social sense. The pioneers were individualists. And they did stand the gaff.

This was the human stuff of America. It was not the stuff one would have chosen to make a nation or an admirable national character. And Americans to-day are the most reckless and lawless of peoples. We are also the most imaginative, the most temperamental, the most infinitely varied people. We are the kindest people on earth; kind every day to one another, and sympathetically responsive to every rumor of distress. It is only in America that a passing car will stop to lend a stranded stranger a tire-tool. Only Americans ever made millions of small personal sacrifices in order to pour wealth over the world, relieving suffering in such distant places as Armenia and Japan.

Everywhere, in shops, streets, factories, elevators, on highways and on farms, Americans are the most friendly and courteous people. There is more laughter and more song in America than anywhere else. Such are a few of the human values that grew from individualism while individualism was creating this nation.

VIII

LOOK at this phenomenon: The United States of America.

For two hundred and fifty years, Europe colonizes this continent. Then Spain holds the Gulf and the Floridas, Mexico, Texas, New Mexico, Arizona and California. Russia is in the north. France controls the Great Lakes and the waterways of the Mississippi valley, the fur trade and the Missouri mines. Along the Atlantic coast, between wilderness and sea, are scattered little English colonies.

Not all the colonies rebel against England. Canada remains loyal to the King, and among the others only Virginia and Massachusetts have any real heart for the fight. The war drags along, a little frontier war fought with valor by a few rebels and neglected by England, whose vital interests are elsewhere. An excursion of French gunboats helps decide the issue. Peace is signed, and thirteen colonies without a common interest do not know whether to unite or to be separate nations.

At this point, what would seem likely to be the future of this continent? Does it seem probable that these colonies, divided by religion, social structure and economic interests, quarreling with each other about over-lapping claims to territory which threaten to break into wars, does it seem probable that they will prevail against the Great Powers already in possession of America's soil? Does it not appear that, if they are merely to survive, they must be united under a most powerful government?

Precisely the opposite occurred. The men who met in Philadelphia to form a government believed that all men are born free. They founded this government on the principle: All power to the individual.

How can such a principle be embodied in government? There is no escape from the fact that any government must be a man, or a few men, in power over the multitude of men. How is it possible to transfer the power of the ruler to each man in this multitude? It is not possible.

This was not a problem merely of allowing common men some voice in the councils of their rulers, some power to stop their rulers in the act of using power to the injury or the robbery of common men. The intent was actually to give the governing power to each common man equally. So that in effect, the political result would be the same as in the Communist village, where each man has equal power and struggles for his own self-interest until a satisfactory balance is arrived at. The governing power of this new republic was actually to reside in the multitudes. Common men were to govern themselves.

But how is it possible to embody this intent in the mechanisms of government, since any government of multitudes of men must be one man, or a few men, in power over the many? It is not possible.

The problem was solved by destroying power itself, so far as this could possibly be done. Power was diminished to an irreducible minimum.

Governing power was broken into three fragments, so that never could any man possess whole power. The function of government was cut into three parts, each checked in action by the other two. Any ruler is a human being, and in a human being thinking, deciding, acting and judging are inseparable. In this government, no man was permitted to function as a whole human being. Congressmen were to think and decide; the executive was to act; the courts were to judge.

And over these three was set a written statement of political principles, to be the strongest check on them all, an impersonal restraint upon the fallible human beings who must be allowed to use these fragments of authority over the multitudes of individuals.

Not without reason, Europeans cried out that this government was anarchy let loose in the world. Not without reason, older governments refused to recognize it. Nearer to anarchy than this, no government can come and be a government. Never before had the multitudes of men been set free to do as they pleased.

Already, a bribed Continental Congress had sold to speculators millions of acres of public lands, claimed by both Connecticut and Virginia. And the first Congress of the United States, with unscrupulous chicanery, robbed the Revolutionary common soldiers of their meager pay and put it in the pockets of Congressmen and New York bankers.

What future could be predicted for such a lack of government, in such a situation?

In seventy years, within a man's lifetime, France and Russia had vanished from this continent. Spain had yielded the Floridas, Texas, New Mexico, Arizona, California. England had been pushed back on the north. The whole vast extent of this country had been covered by one nation, a tumultuous multitude of men under the weakest government in the world. How did this happen?

The characteristic of American history is that everything appears to happen by accident. Nothing seems planned or intended. Other nations adopt policies and pursue them; their history is formed by the clash of these policies with other planned policies elsewhere. But America moves by a kind of indirection. Always in these United States the unintended, the apparently irrational, happens.

Consider the gain of that vast block of territory between the Ohio river and the Great Lakes, the Mississippi and the sea-coast colonies. One man did that; George Rogers Clark. He borrowed the money and got most of his men from the Spanish governor and the French people of Missouri and Illinois; he made one of the most terrible winter marches in history, and captured in Vincennes the commander of British forces in the West. No one had planned to do it, no one but George Rogers Clark and his little band knew it was being done.

By that one independent stroke, a free and enterprising American destroyed a plan which had been carefully matured for two years in London and in Canada. He took the United States to the Mississippi. And neither the Virginia Assembly nor the Congress of the United States ever paid the drafts he had given in St. Louis for the military supplies he used. Those drafts were not paid; George Rogers Clark was ruined, the Spanish governor was ruined, the fur-

traders of St. Louis took a frightful loss and one great
fur-trading house collapsed, because they were not
paid. But the United States had the Northwest
Territory.

Consider the settlement of Kentucky. Henderson's
land company did that. The government wished
to curb and restrain western settlement; it went too
fast, it was too lawless, it threatened rebellion against
the United States and trouble with Spain. Any intelligent man in power would have stopped it. But
there was no man in power, because there was no
power that any man could use. And Judge Henderson saw a chance to make a fortune.

He sold Kentucky land to the settlers, on credit,
and he would have made a fortune if they had paid
for it. They didn't; they drove off his installment
collectors with guns. The Henderson land company
failed in the depression of the 1790's. But Kentucky
was settled.

Consider the Louisiana Purchase, which took the
United States from the Mississippi to the Rocky
Mountains. No one had any intention of buying
that land. Everyone saw the Mississippi as the permanent frontier of the United States. The great river
was a natural geographical boundary.

As had been foreseen, however, Kentucky was
making trouble. Those western settlers threatened
to join Spain, which held the Gulf and kept them
from a sea-port. Jefferson saw that the whole West
— that is to say, the eastern half of the Mississippi
valley — would be lost unless the United States could

get a port on the Gulf. All that he wanted was a port, just one little bay.

Two American commissioners in Paris, with no authority whatever to do so, bought the whole of Louisiana from Napoleon. It belonged to Spain, but Napoleon sold it; his armies could settle the matter with Spain. And two Americans bought it, paid fifteen million dollars for it. Jefferson was aghast when he heard the news. He came within an inch of repudiating the purchase.

Consider a question as vital as slavery. Everywhere else in the western world, slavery was abolished by deliberate, well-considered legislation or decree. Every time the question was submitted to Americans, an overwhelming majority voted against abolishing slavery.

Then Lincoln was elected on a platform promising free land and a railroad to the Pacific. An old quarrel about division of power between state and Federal governments blazed at last into a war which had been narrowly averted for half a century, and, as a war measure, slavery was abolished.

No one intended to drive the Indians from the Middle West. Again and again, in good faith, United States treaties established Indian tribes forever as permanent buffer states. That was a rational policy, based upon all future probabilities that could be seen at the time. Again and again, Federal troops evicted white settlers from lands secured by treaty to the Indians. But there was no control over individualism, and the Indians vanished.

California was torn from Mexico, as a surreptitious personal adventure of General Fremont's, connived in by Senator Benton of Missouri who sent him word to move quickly before he was stopped. It was done at a time when no one dreamed there was gold in those foothills and thoughtful men knew that California's soil was worthless because the United States already had far more land than Americans could use, and for centuries to come the population on the Pacific coast would not be large enough to be a market for farm products.

Aroused by selfish, private propaganda and inspired by democratic ideals, Americans rushed to war to free Cuba from Spain's imperial tyranny, and found that they were fighting the Filipinos to keep them from freeing themselves. Thus the United States became an empire and a world power.

Such instances are multiplied by hundreds, by thousands. Everywhere you look at American history you see them. There is no plan, no intention, no fixed policy anywhere; this is anarchy, this is chaos. It is individualism. In less than a century, it created our America.

IX

FOR seven years I have been looking at America. I had spent more than thirty years in my own country, before; I had traveled over it everywhere and had lived in many of its states, but I had never seen it. Americans should look at America. Look at this vast, infinitely various, completely unstandardized, complex, subtle, passionate, strong, weak, beautiful, inorganic and intensely vital land.

How could we be so bemused by books and by the desire of our own minds to make a pattern, as to apply to these United States the ideology of Europe?

With some rough approximation to fact, Europeans can think in terms of Labor, Capital, System, and The State. One can speak of Labor in Paris, where the working class is rigidly distinct from other classes; in England, where their very speech, their clothing and their schooling set them apart; in Rome, where workingmen are proud to know that even a workingman's ordained life serves Italy, and in Venice where only the son of a gondolier has ever been permitted to become a gondolier.

Capitalist is a word of some meaning in those countries where, within a social framework only slightly shaken, men with money have climbed to those upper levels held yesterday by the aristocrat. There is a profit system, where business has seeped into and replaced the feudal system. The State is a shorthand symbol for many facts, where bureaucracies control a regimented social-economic order.

In America a man works, but he is not Labor. A hundred million men, working, are not Labor. They are a hundred million individuals with a hundred million backgrounds, characters, tastes, ambitions and degrees of ability. Each of them, amid the uncertainties, dangers, risks, opportunities and catastrophes of an inorganic society, creates his own life and his own status as best he can.

An American raises wheat, but he is not The

Wheatgrower. In every state of this union, men of every race and circumstance and mind, by every possible variety of method and with many varying needs and many ends in view, raise wheat. All of them together are not The Wheatgrower. Men raise cotton, men grow oranges, men plant soybeans; they are not Agriculture.

Agriculture, used as a word applied to human beings, means a class of men attached to the soil. There is no such class in America. Excepting only the old landed aristocracy of the South, which was already vanishing when Lincoln was born, there has never been such a class in this country. From the first, Americans were gamblers, speculators. They gambled in land when the gambling was good in land; they were never genuinely attached to the soil, to one bit of earth, these fields, this woodland, this stream, this sky, these changing seasons that became their own because they loved them and their life was in them. There is the European Peasant; there is no American Farmer.

An American farms if he hopes to make money farming. He sells his land when he can sell it at a profit. He mortgages it, if he thinks he can buy more land on a rising market, or get into a good gamble in wheat, oil, mines, live-stock or Wall Street. On a falling market, he gets out from under if he can, and runs a filling station, sells automobiles, starts a grocery store or a restaurant. His son may become anything, from a Dillinger to a Henry Ford of the future.

The Capitalist can not be found; he does not exist. Men of many different minds and for many purposes, or by accident or luck or the skill of a pirate, create huge business and financial organizations, and fight to make them bigger and to draw bigger profits from them. But here everything is fluid, changing and uncertain; nothing is static and secure. Here is no solidly established class, placed in a social order and holding lower classes steady like cows to be milked. To capture control over the American multitudes is not possible, because no control exists to be captured.

As long as our form of government stands, there can be no such control. Every business and financial undertaking must serve the unpredictable multitudes of common men, and swiftly change to serve their changing demands and desires, tomorrow and tomorrow and tomorrow, or rivals will rise from those multitudes and destroy it.

Ownership must constantly be fought for and defended, and in this very struggle ownership of the great corporations has melted away; it has become so scattered and diffused through the multitudes that no one can say where it begins or ends, and the ultimate destination of profits from industry, if there be one, cannot be discovered.

Economic interests intermingle, the debtor is also the creditor, the producer is the consumer, the insurance company raises wheat, the farmer is selling short on the Board of Trade. Everything meets itself coming and going; no one can understand it, and every picture made neat and orderly against this chaos is false.

A few thousand men in this struggle and confusion

apparently possess enormous sums of money. But look for this money and it is not there; it is not solid actuality; it is not the tangible property, unmortgaged and secure, of a *rentier* class, nor the Junker's hold on vast stretches of earth and many villages. It is dynamic power pouring through business and industry, and like the power that drives a machine, if it is stopped it vanishes.

These vast fortunes exist only as dynamic power, and this power, too, must serve the multitudes. American wealth is innumerable streams of power, fed by small sources and great ones, flowing through the mechanisms that produce the vast quantities of goods consumed by the multitudes, and the men who are called the owners can hardly be said even to control the wealth that stands recorded as theirs, for its very existence depends upon satisfying chaotic wants and pleasing unpredictable tastes. Fortunes that were making good hairpins vanished when American women cut their hair.

Some thousands of men in America direct fragments of economic power as best they can, and these men draw out of the streams of this dynamic power as much tangible wealth as they and their families can consume. Many of them draw out huge sums, beyond any man's power to consume, and use these sums to build libraries, hospitals, museums, or for unique and inestimable service to music, science, public health.

Many of them spend stupidly and wastefully as much as can possibly be spent in the most luxurious and decadent manners of living, and this spectacle is infuriating. Many a time when my bills and my debts have been piling up and my most frantic efforts have failed to dig a dollar or any hope out of this chaos, so that the nights were harder to live through than the desperate days, I have thought of those jeweled women carelessly dripping handfuls of gold pieces on the tables at Monte Carlo, of those quite charming necklaces worth a hundred thousand dollars and the fur coats for only $25,000. Did I say, infuriating? The word is mild.

I was once at heart a revolutionist, and you can tell me nothing about poverty, nothing about the suffering, the injustices, the hunger, the apparently needless cruelties that exist from coast to coast of this country. But you can tell me no longer that they are the result of a capitalistic system, because there is no system here.

All these men, who in various ways, for various purposes and with widely varying results to the welfare and happiness of others, struggle to direct American industry, are expensive. They are expensive, in that they draw large amounts of actual money from the streams of productive power and pour these sums back into the streams again by spending them for their own individual purposes—often purely selfish purposes.

But if this chaos were replaced by a system, a social order so perfect that there would be no trace of selfishness in it, an order perfectly functioning for the sole purpose of serving the public good, these men must be replaced by a bureaucracy. And a bureaucracy is expensive, too.

The bureaucracy that is necessary to controlling in

detail, and according to a plan devised by men possessing centralized economic power, all the processes of business, industry, finance and agriculture in a modern state, is stupendously expensive.

Such a bureaucracy is costly not only in ever-increasing pay-rolls but in human energy. For it must take great and ever-increasing numbers of men from productive activity and set them to dreary work amid coils of red tape and masses of papers recording what other men have done and may perhaps be permitted to do, and ordered to do.

Also, bureaucracies are stupid and sluggish impediments to the whole range of human activities, as anyone knows who has struggled to move under their clogging weight in Europe. Bureaucracies slow down, impede and postpone the realization of the multitude's desires, because they are not compelled, as in this American chaos business and industry are compelled, to serve those desires or perish.

x

THIS American chaos of released human energies has been going on for little more than a century, less than half of this country's past history. In that time it has created America and made America the richest country in the world. Where has this wealth come from?

Americans have been exploiting the natural resources of half a continent. And this exploitation is continuing now and should resume its accelerating rate of speed, for our unused natural wealth is enormous. Electric power, for instance, has hardly begun to be exploited. But natural resources alone do not explain our relatively greater wealth, for while Americans have been exploiting America, Europeans have been exploiting Asia, Africa, South America, the East Indies, the West Indies, Australia and the South Seas.

No such riches poured into American hands as Mexico and Peru gave Spain. There are mines in Burma, China, old Russia and Australia as well as in Nevada. California's gold did not equal South Africa's gold and diamonds. There are coal and iron in Britain and in the Saar, almost inexhaustible oil in Persia, Mosul, Azerbaijan and Venezuela. The great forests of the world were not in America. No soil on earth is as productive as Egypt and the Soudan. Coffee, rubber, sugar, rum, spices and copra and tin paid dividends. India returned some profit, and Indo-China has not been a loss to France, nor the East Indies to the Netherlands. I find it difficult to see that Americans have been exploiting more natural resources than Europeans have.

Free land will not explain our wealth. Wealth comes not from land, but from labor on the land, and subject populations toil perhaps even more industriously than free men. Incidentally, it is an error to suppose that land in this country cost nothing.

Big speculators grabbed this soil, on credit, and sold it for high prices. The fury of speculation in land-warrants began before our government was created. The Continental Congress, in one deal, sold five million acres in Ohio. Virginia sold, in blocks of a thousand acres, Kentucky, the Carolinas, Mississippi, Tennessee, and no one knew how much of Ohio, Indiana and Illinois. That speculating crashed in the 1790's, with business failures and hard times.

After the Louisiana Purchase, when the wage for twelve hours' hard work was twenty-five cents, the United States Land Office in one year sold five million acre of Missouri river-bottom land at an average price of five dollars an acre. Speculators got it, and prices jumped. Speculation went mad over town lots; promoters sold them for $50; they jumped to $250., $500., $800., $1,000. Farm land went to $50. an acre. The bottom dropped out in the bank-crash of 1819.

The Homestead Act was passed in 1862, when only the supposedly uninhabitable Great American Desert remained. Twenty-eight years later the last of the Great American Desert was seized in the last land-run. Two decades after that, I myself helped to sell the virgin land of California for prices ranging to $800. an acre.

Perhaps America is the richest country because Americans did seize so much territory and make it one country with no trade-barriers across it. Perhaps it is the richest country because Americans welcomed and exploited the industrial revolution, applied science and the machines, as no other people did. And perhaps they were able to do this because they were not hampered by frontiers, class distinctions and the weight of bureaucracies, as Europeans have always been.

The fact that America is the richest country is not

alone so important; England is rich, and so are France
and the Netherlands; so was pre-war Germany, and
the Austrian empire. It is more important that the
United States of America is the country of the richest
population in the world.

Logically, unrestrained selfishness should build up
vast wealth for a few, and submerge the multitudes
into more miserable poverty. The logical Germanic
mind of Marx saw that. He saw and could statistically
count a certain amount of wealth, tangible, solid as an
apple. It followed naturally that the more of it was
seized by the upper class, the less would be left for
the lower classes. The rich would grow richer and
the poor, poorer.

Actually, in this country the opposite occurred.
In enjoyment of wealth there is less disparity, now,
today, between the richest American and the average
American workingman than there was between Jefferson at Monticello and the average far western settler
in Kentucky.

It appears that individualism tends to a leveling of
wealth, to destroying economic inequality. Marx, the
European, had no conception of the enormous creative energies released when multitudes of men, for
the first time freed from economic control, set out
each in his own way to get for himself the greatest
possible amount of wealth. Certainly this brief experiment in individualism has not only created great
wealth and an unimaginable multiplication of forms
of wealth in goods and services, but it has also distributed these forms of wealth to an unprecedented
and elsewhere unequalled degree. We express this

by saying that America has the highest standard of living in the world.

This, too, seems to have happened by accident. We all know that it was not planned; no one intended it. Each of us has been out to get all he could for himself and his family, "upon the simple rule and good old plan that he shall take who has the power, and he shall keep who can."

XI

ONLY once have any large number of Americans wanted to distribute wealth, and they did not intend to raise the standard of living. The standard of living had already risen too high and crashed too deplorably. They wanted to return to the prosperity of the 80's.

This happened forty years ago. I remember it well. Hard times had ended forever an age of enormous expansion in business, finance, invention and wealth. Within the memory of my parents, who were not old, living conditions had been utterly transformed.

The kerosene lamp had replaced candles and the work of candlemaking; the spinning wheel was gone, the loom was used now only for making rag carpets. Machine-made cloth, machine-made shoes, factory-made brooms had thrown men out of work, but with boughten soap and baking powder they had revolutionized housekeeping. Wire nails, wire fence, riding plows, mowing machines and binders, eight-horse threshers, had made farming easy — easier, in fact, than it is today in Europe.

Railroads ran from coast to coast, postal service was

fast and cheap, base-burners warmed the parlors, the telegraph had gone almost everywhere. In those piping days, business boomed. On Fifth Avenue rose the gas-lit palaces of — almost incredible, but true — of millionaires. In the Middle West women wore silk on Sundays; men smoked good cigars and drove fast teams. Then suddenly, crash! the Panic.

Some blamed the tariff, more blamed the railroads. (In 1860, a majority at the polls had demanded subsidies for railroads. It might have been better for the railroads if they had had no government help; in 1890 and thereafter they were bitterly hated because they were subsidized. The hatred lasted until those enemies of the people were curbed, regulated and controlled by the Interstate Commerce Commission.)

Everyone was in debt, of course. There has been no time since the founding of this republic when Americans were not deeply in debt. Mortgages were foreclosed, banks failed, factories shut down, farm prices slumped. Charitable ladies opened soup kitchens in the cities. Farmers, after creditors took the cow, could live on potatoes and turnips until the mortgage took the farm.

A population shaken from the soil moved along the roads in covered wagons drawn by hungry horses. Organized bands of unemployed swarmed from the cities, shouting, "We have the bone and sinew! We demand our rights as working men!" City police and the militia had driven them from the closed factories and the city streets. They terrorized small towns.

From the Pacific to the Mississippi they captured

trains, crowded the cars, and cheered unemployed train crews taking them full-speed eastward. Traffic was demoralized. From the Mississippi eastward, dispatchers cleared all trains off their divisions. From the Mississippi, Coxey's Army of the unemployed marched on foot to Washington. Federal troops guarded government buildings.

It is all in the files of old newspapers, for those who do not remember so long ago. I was riding in a covered wagon and listening by the campfires, and I remember.

Meanwhile most families went on living undramatically, as most families always do everywhere, through depression, inflation, revolution and war. Very few persons starved to death. Someone in America will always divide food with the desperately hungry. It may be that American kindness had grown from each American's sense of insecurity.

But starvation, or even the general malnutrition during those years which semi-starved so many children, is not the worst of poverty among an individualistic people. In this country poverty is not the chronic state of certain classes, to be borne as animals bear cold, so that it is a physical thing. Normal Americans feel an individual responsibility, a necessity to think, act, achieve; poverty from which we can find no escape is an agony of mind and spirit. We blame ourselves, we feel our self-respect mortally wounded, we suffer.

After three years of such suffering, most Americans knew what they wanted. They wanted to destroy The Trusts.

The Trusts were the grandparents of our present huge corporations. We saw them as combinations in restraint of trade. Trade, business, had been good in the 8o's; now it was stagnant, it had stopped; obviously something was stopping it, and all our bright, popular economists saw that our enemy was The Trusts. Statistics proved this, and so did our experience, for everyone had been prosperous while The Trusts were forming, and now that The Trusts were solidly there, everyone was poor.

Everyone, that is, was poor, except the few men who owned The Trusts. A few men did actually own and control them, for they were new and the melting-away of ownership had hardly begun. These few men actually owned, or appeared to own, as much as a million dollars apiece. In a word, they had all the money in the country.

There was no more free land. Farmers could not make money enough to pay taxes. There were no jobs; the factories were closed. And less than ten-percent of the population owned more than 90 percent of the wealth. Rich women were pampering pug dogs, while children were starving. Something must be done.

"Bust the Trusts!" we shouted. Our champion against them was the silver-tongued boy-orator from the Platte, William Jennings Bryan.

William Jennings Bryan fearlessly came out of the West to fight for The Common Man. He faced the intrenched cohorts of selfishness whose only thought was their bloated money-bags, and defied them in the name of suffering Humanity.

"You shall not press down upon the brow of Labor this crown of thorns!" he thundered. "You shall not crucify mankind upon a cross of gold!"

He was an economist. He proposed to curb and restrain The Trusts by the free coinage of silver, at a ratio to gold of 16-to-1. The arguments were involved and difficult to follow, but Bryan's heart was in the right place and, with all sincerity, it was bleeding for the suffering people and the dangerous state of our country.

That was the fiercest political battle in the history of this republic. The masses of the people were furiously determined to destroy The Trusts, and it was quite true that currency inflation would have ruined them; also, of course, it would have destroyed utterly the value of all money, no matter whose.

Rich men had actual power then and naturally they defended their money. They fought for it openly and fiercely, and by the narrowest margin they saved it. They defeated Bryan. The multitudes of Americans had made their one effort to distribute wealth, and had failed.

Yet wealth has so increasingly been created and distributed that today, harassed as we are by personal anxieties and seriously alarmed by the public debt, few Americans would think of refusing help from public funds to any family as destitute of proper food, clothing, shelter, medical care and financial safety as the majority of American families were then.

XII

TWENTY-FIVE years ago, high schools were rare. To-day America, and only America, offers every child free schooling from infancy to the university degree. Only America has a free public-library system, with an extension service to every village and farm. Only America has free radio programs and unlicenced, un-taxed radios. Common men elsewhere do not think of owning a radio. Except the British empire, only America has an uncensored press.

The telephone, the electric light, the silk stocking, fresh vegetables and fruits in winter, sanitary meat markets, the ice-box, and the milk-bottle, the gas range and the kerosene cookstove, ready-made clothes, the seamless sheet, wall-paper, the toothbrush, the leather shoe, moving pictures, ice-cream, and a thousand other things to which Americans are so accustomed that we do not see them, all testify to such a distribution of wealth in this individualistic country as no other people have dreamed of enjoying.

Twenty-five years ago, the automobile was a rich man's prerogative. It still is, everywhere but here. In America, the anarchy of uncontrolled individual-istic selfishness has so distributed automobiles that California is overwhelmed by scores of thousands of penniless families arriving in them, and hunger march-ers do not march but travel in trucks. And these people should have automobiles; that is precisely my point. They should have them, and individualism has somehow, without plan or any such definite pur-pose, seen to it that they do have them.

Twenty-five years ago a majority of Americans bathed in the washtub on Saturday nights and lighted their way to bed with a kerosene lamp. The English are still renowned throughout the world for their extraordinary personal cleanliness, because in every English middle-class home or upper middle-class London hotel a bath can be had in a tin tub carried to the bedroom. Today our American intellectuals point indignantly to an America which has left more than two million farm houses without modern bathrooms or electric lights. Something, they say, must be done about this.

There must be more than two million American families who still use the washtub and the kerosene lamp. They should have plumbing and electricity. They should have automatic central heat, electric refrigeration, air-conditioning, television, and every other form of material wealth that may be imagined and created to serve them in the future.

There is still far too much economic inequality; the gap between rich and poor has not been sufficiently narrowed. Something certainly should be done to distribute wealth, to raise the general standard of living, to improve living conditions for the poor and to give everyone, particularly the rich, a more abundant life.

But that is precisely what this anarchy of individualism has been doing, increasingly doing for the brief time in modern history during which it has been operating. When I look at this unique American experiment which has barely begun, which has been progressing for hardly a century and a half, I think it can stand on its record.

XIII

WE look too much at charts and statistics. We would learn more by looking at America.

Oddly enough, statistics appear only in times of agitation and distress. Their function would appear to be that of omens of worse to come. We seem to have a morbid taste for them, like that of children for ghost-stories that raise the hair. The American air has not been so full of fragmentary statistics since the Panic of 1893.

I read again, for instance, that less than ten percent of our population own more than ninety percent of the wealth. This alarmed me in 1893.

I read also that a hundred years ago 80 percent of our population owned property, and that today the percentage is 23. Such an expropriation, if it has occurred, is alarming. But it seems to me even more alarming that many American minds accept this statement as true upon no better proof than that they have read it, and from it conclude, first, that "something must be done," and second, that the proper thing to do is to take ownership away from individuals and have property administered by The State; which means, by autocratic rulers giving orders through an enormous bureaucracy.

When I look at America, I do not see that more than three citizens in four are destitute of property.

What I see is that the forms of property have changed. I suspect that if any trained statistician would state that nearly four in five of us own no property, he would be speaking of forms of property known as "real property" a hundred years ago.

Fewer men own farms, because better transportation and refrigerator cars have made it possible to deliver good food to large populations in cities and because improved farm machinery makes larger acreages inevitable. Fewer men own houses, because many prefer to rent apartments. Almost all the thousands of little factories, worked by a family and a neighbor's son or two, and all the little water-mills grinding corn and wheat, and making paper, have disappeared. On the streams of America there are no longer the little potato-starch factories, and the cracker-factories, and the saw mills. In statistics it will appear that the Great Biscuit Company, one owner, has replaced five thousand owners of little cracker factories.

Yet how many men, a hundred years ago, owned endowment insurance policies? or a share in a building-and-loan association? or a few shares of Great Biscuit Company stock? or an automobile, a radio, an electric refrigerator and a typewriter? The fact is that in statistics I myself appear as one of the dispossessed, and I know a dozen persons who pay income taxes and own no "real property" whatever.

Looking at America, I wonder also about the statistical percentage of Americans who are somehow existing on an income below the "line of subsistence."

I live in a farmhouse near a village of 800 people,

in a submarginal farming region in the Ozarks, techni-
cally known as rural slums. The upstanding, de-
cidedly self-respecting Americans whose homes are
these clean frame houses, warmed by stoves, lighted
by kerosene, have no idea that they live in slums.
They live as their fathers lived, and they like it.
Every time they bundle their families into the car and
drive to California, or Texas or Idaho, they return
saying there's no place like home.

They like fresh, cold water bubbling out of the
rock, and watermelons cooled in the spring. They
enjoy fox-chases, and fiddling, and basket dinners.
Forty years ago they needed no "cash money" whatever except to pay their taxes. Today they have
plenty to eat and room to shelter their relatives whose
jobs have failed in the cities, and though they feel the
pinch of taxes, they get along all right on a very few
dollars a week from cream-checks.

In the town, there are not sixty persons who would
appear in statistics above the "line of subsistence."
In the whole county, only eight incomes are above
the $1000. a year which shows on income-tax returns.

Yet this village has electric lights, a water and a
sewer system, telephones of course, and a paved main
street brilliant at night with Neon signs. The village
offers every child free schooling through high school,
and brings the country children to it in free buses.
We get first run moving pictures often before New
York does. Our Beauty Shop has the latest equip-
ment for facials, manicures, permanent waves.

With not twenty exceptions, the houses are pretty
little houses, bungalows and stone cottages, well cared

for, with lawns and foundation plantings, plumbing, ice boxes, telephones, radios. There are a number of electric refrigerators in town, and several electric ranges, though many women still use blue-flame kerosene ranges. Nearly every family has a car. The washerwomen use electric washing machines. Most of the men wear overalls except when they dress up, but you will find no more tasteful or more smartly worn clothes than the women's inexpensive dresses. They all wear silk stockings, of course.

This village is no exception. Drive along the highways and you pass through such villages every few miles. A large part of the population of all of them is below the statistical line of subsistence.

I gather from these observed facts that there must be some millions of men and women in this country who, on paper, appear as in the direst need of rehabilitation, and who would be mortally offended if you told them so.

XIV

THERE is nothing new in planned and controlled economy. Human beings have lived under various forms of that social security for six thousand years. The new thing is the anarchy of individualism, which has been operating freely only in this country for a century and a half.

I look at it now, and ask myself whether individualism has enough social vitality to survive in a world turning back to the essentially medieval, static forms. Can individualism, which by its very nature has no

organization and no leader, stand against the determined attack of a small group, organized, controlled,
and fanatically sure that a strong man in power can
give a people better lives than they can create for
themselves?

The spirit of individualism is still here. There are
about a quarter of a billion human beings in these
United States, and not one of us has escaped anxiety,
and very few of us have not been forced to reduce our
standard of living during these past few years. The
number of us who have been out of work and facing
actual hunger is not known; the largest estimate has
been twelve million. Of this number, barely a third
have appeared on the reported relief rolls. Somewhere those millions in need of help, who have not
been helped, are still, like the rest of us, fighting
through this depression on their own.

Millions of farmers are still lords on their own land;
they are not receiving checks from the public funds to
which they contribute their increasing taxes.

Millions of men and women have quietly been paying debts from which they asked no release; millions
have cut expenses to the barest necessities, spending
every dime in fear that soon they will have nothing,
and somehow being cheerful in the daytime and finding God knows what strength or weakness in themselves during the black nights.

Americans are still paying the price of individual
liberty, which is individual responsibility and insecurity.

These unnoticed Americans are defending the
principle on which this republic was founded,

the principle that created this country and has, in fact, brought the greatest good to the greatest number. By such courage and endurance, the American principle has been successfully defended, time after time, for more than a century.

We remember the Americans who died in the wars of this country. We build memorials to their memory and lay flowers on their graves. It was the Americans who lived and kept their fighting spirit through the hard and bitter times that followed every surge of prosperity, it was men and women who cared enough for their own personal freedom to take the risks of self-reliance and starve if they could not feed themselves, who created our country, the free country, the richest and the happiest country in the world.

But during that first century, the western world was turning toward democracy. The test of strength comes now, when half of Europe has definitely turned back from democracy to the old stability in which the multitudes, having no authority, have no responsibility, but leave both the power and the burden to their rulers.

Printed in the United States
111558LV00005B/310/A